TAYLOR

V.

PINNACLE PACKAGING PRODUCTS, INC.

Third Edition

Trial Materials

D1737441

TAYLOR

V.

PINNACLE PACKAGING PRODUCTS, INC.

Third Edition

Trial Materials

Hon. Andrew P. Rodovich

Thomas J. Leach
University of the Pacific
McGeorge School of Law

NITA®
NATIONAL INSTITUTE FOR TRIAL ADVOCACY

Address inquiries to:

Reprint Permission
National Institute for Trial Advocacy
1685 38th Street, Suite 200
Boulder, CO 80301-2735
Phone: (800) 225-6482
Fax: (720) 890-7069
Email: permissions@nita.org

ISBN 978-1-60156-445-0 (print)
eISBN 978-1-63282-215-4 (eBook)
FBA 1445

Printed in the United States of America

 Wolters Kluwer

Official co-publisher of NITA.
WKLegaledu.com/NITA

CONTENTS

INTRODUCTION

On May 11, YR-2, the plaintiff, Jamie Taylor, was hired by the defendant, Pinnacle Packaging Products Inc., to work in the warehouse. Pursuant to company policy, the plaintiff was considered a probationary employee for sixty days. The plaintiff was fired by the warehouse manager, John Hamilton, on June 22, YR-2. The plaintiff alleges that she was fired because she resisted Hamilton's advances.

The applicable law is contained in the final instructions at the end of the case file.

The plaintiff's witnesses at trial will include:

Jamie Taylor

Lisa Roberts

Jerry Black

The defendant's witnesses at trial will include:

John Hamilton

Chuck Singleton

Michelle Johnson

Janet Long

Electronic exhibits can be found at the following website:

http://bit.ly/1P20Jea
Password: Taylor3trial

UNITED STATES DISTRICT COURT

NORTHERN DISTRICT OF NITA

DARROW DIVISION

Jamie TAYLOR,
Plaintiff

          :
          :
          :

v.   :   CAUSE NO. YR-1 cv 321

          :

PINNACLE PACKAGING PRODUCTS   :   JURY DEMAND
INC.,   :
Defendant   :

COMPLAINT

Comes now the Plaintiff, Jamie Taylor, and for cause of action against the Defendant, Pinnacle Packaging Products Inc., alleges:

1. On May 11, YR-2, the Plaintiff was hired to work on the packaging line in the warehouse of the Defendant.

2. During her employment, the Plaintiff was sexually harassed by the warehouse manager, John Hamilton, who repeatedly asked the Plaintiff to go out with him.

3. When the Plaintiff refused the sexual advances of Hamilton, she was terminated without cause on June 22, YR-2.

4. The Plaintiff timely filed a charge with the Equal Employment Opportunity Commission and received a right to sue letter within the last ninety days.

WHEREFORE the Plaintiff, Jamie Taylor, DEMANDS judgment against the Defendant, Pinnacle Packaging Products Inc., for compensatory damages and all other appropriate relief.

Filed: 2/11/YR-1

Maurie Howard
_____
Attorney for Plaintiff

UNITED STATES DISTRICT COURT
NORTHERN DISTRICT OF NITA
DARROW DIVISION

Jamie TAYLOR, Plaintiff	:	
	:	
v.	:	CAUSE NO. YR-1 cv 321
	:	
PINNACLE PACKAGING PRODUCTS INC., Defendant	:	JURY DEMAND

ANSWER TO COMPLAINT

Comes now the Defendant, Pinnacle Packaging Products Inc., and in answer to the Plaintiff's complaint states:

1. Admit.

2. Deny.

3. Defendant admits that the Plaintiff was terminated on June 22, YR-2, but denies the remaining allegations of paragraph 3.

4. Admit.

Wherefore, the Defendant, Pinnacle Packaging Products Inc., demands judgment against the Plaintiff, Jamie Taylor, and for all other appropriate relief.

AFFIRMATIVE DEFENSE

Comes now the Defendant, Pinnacle Packaging Products Inc., and for an affirmative defense states that it had a company policy against all forms of sex discrimination and that the Plaintiff unreasonably failed to follow that policy and report any instances of sexual harassment.

Filed: 3/5/YR-1

_____
Attorney for Defendant

DEPOSITIONS

DEPOSITION OF JAMIE TAYLOR

My name is Jamie Taylor, and my date of birth is March 21, YR-23. I have a high school diploma, and I have had several jobs since high school. In May YR-2, my friend, Lisa Roberts, told me that her company, Pinnacle Packaging Products, was looking for some people to work on the packaging line in the warehouse. Lisa and I have been friends since high school, and she got me a job application from the warehouse manager, John Hamilton. I submitted my application and was hired after an interview with Hamilton.

My first day of work was May 11, YR-2. I was scheduled to work the 8:00 a.m. to 4:30 p.m. shift. All new employees have a probationary status for sixty days. I was paid $9.50 per hour and was scheduled to work a forty-hour week. After my probationary status was completed, I would have received medical insurance and other benefits. I started working on a packaging line, and my immediate foreman was Chuck Singleton. I started work on Monday, and the first week went without incident.

Because Friday was Singleton's birthday, several employees on our lines decided to take him out for drinks after work. We went to Kool's Korner, about one mile from the company. I had ridden to work with Lisa all week, so she drove me to Kool's Korner. About twenty people showed up after work, and we all were standing around because there were not enough seats for everyone. Some people stayed for one or two drinks, and only seven or eight of us were left by 7:00 p.m. Lisa and I pushed two tables together and sat down.

Hamilton had arrived at Kool's Korner about one hour after everyone else, and I had not talked to him that evening. I was a little surprised when he sat down next to me. Of course, Singleton was still there, and he sat across the table from Hamilton.

We all talked for another hour, and Hamilton bought a round of drinks for the table. By this time, I believe that I had four drinks. I felt a little light-headed because I was drinking on an empty stomach. Lisa was having a good time, and her boyfriend, Mark Stewart, had joined the party and was sitting next to Lisa. It did not appear as though she would be leaving anytime soon.

The dress code of Pinnacle is casual, and I was wearing a pair of jeans and a sweatshirt. Because Lisa was talking to Mark, I spent most of my time talking to Hamilton and Singleton. Without warning, Hamilton put his hand on my knee. I did not know what to do, so I did not say anything. I tried to act like nothing was happening and continued our conversation. Apparently, Hamilton was encouraged because I had not done anything, so he moved his hand a little further up my thigh. I moved closer to Lisa and turned my leg, and his hand came off my leg.

I was anxious to leave the bar and asked Lisa when she was going home. She had just ordered another drink, and Lisa said she would leave when she finished it. Hamilton told me that he was planning on leaving and asked me whether I wanted a ride home. I was reluctant to leave with him, but I did not want to wait around for Lisa. I told Hamilton that I would accept the ride from him.

I live at 1234 Main Street, which is about three miles from Kool's Korner. There are eight apartments in my building, and my apartment overlooks Main Street. Hamilton did not say anything on the ride home that concerned me. When we stopped in front of my apartment building, he started to tell me that I was doing a good job at work. He also said that I would get a raise when I completed my probationary period. He told me that Singleton made recommendations on who was promoted but that he had the final say.

As he was talking to me, he put his hand on my knee again. I was concerned because we were alone and the street was not well lit. I did not pull away, but I told him that I had to leave because I had to get up early on Saturday. Hamilton then leaned over and kissed me good night. I was so surprised that I did not resist or try to push him away. I quickly said good night and got out of his car. When I got inside, I called Lisa on her cell phone to tell her what had happened. She still was at the bar, and I could tell that she was having a good time. She laughed it off and commented that he was not the worst guy I had been out with. I told Lisa that I would see her Monday morning.

On May 18, YR-2, I returned to work for the 8:00 a.m. shift. I saw Hamilton in his office talking to Singleton. Hamilton's office is near the employee entrance to the warehouse. The front wall of his office is mostly glass. The lower three feet is made of concrete blocks, and everything else is windows. I tried not to look into the office and walked directly to my work site.

Hamilton normally walks through the warehouse several times during the shift. Sometimes he stops and talks to a worker or Singleton, and other times he watches what is going on before returning to his office. Around 9:30 a.m., Hamilton walked up to me and asked whether I had a good weekend. He did not talk long, and neither one of us said anything about Friday evening. Later that day, Singleton moved my work station over to in front of the window into Hamilton's office, which I thought was strange—what were they watching me so closely for? Exhibit 11 is an accurate diagram of the warehouse, and I have marked it to show my two different work stations.

I did not have any problems with Singleton during my first week on the job. On Monday, Singleton criticized me for not working fast enough and for taking too many bathroom breaks. Hamilton did not say anything to me about my job performance on Monday, and he only stopped to talk to me that one time in the morning.

The criticism that started on Monday continued during the rest of the week. It seemed like Singleton was watching me all the time and waiting for something to complain about. Lisa did not work on the same packaging line, but I complained to her about Singleton.

When I returned to work on Monday, May 25, YR-2, Singleton was waiting for me with a written reprimand. It stated that I spent too much time away from my work station and that I was not meeting the production quotas. He also told me that I had to meet with Hamilton before starting work.

Singleton and I waited in Hamilton's office for him to arrive. Shortly after 8:00 a.m., Hamilton came in, and Singleton gave him a copy of the reprimand. Hamilton read the write-up and reminded me that I was on probation. He also said that any additional write-ups would affect his decision on whether I would become a full-time employee.

Singleton and I started to leave the office when Hamilton told me that I had to sign the reprimand. I signed it and gave it back to him. Before I could leave the office, Hamilton told me that I was much prettier when I smiled. I told him that I did not feel like smiling, and he said that I should not worry about my job. As I turned to leave, Hamilton asked me whether I would join him for a few drinks after work. I told him that I did not think that it was a good idea.

I went directly to my work station, and I could tell Singleton was irritated by the delay in Hamilton's office. I worked as hard as I could, especially when Singleton was around.

Hamilton made his usual rounds on Monday. The first few times, he ignored me. I was convinced that he was mad at me. When he walked past me during the afternoon, I said hello and asked him how he was doing. He stopped to talk to me for a few minutes before he moved on through the warehouse.

The warehouse is not air conditioned and sometimes can get very warm. In late May, the weather was getting very warm. All of the employees dress casually, and both the men and women started wearing T-shirts. I did not think my T-shirts were too tight or suggestive.

On May 26, YR-2, Singleton complained about my outfit for the first time. It was hot in the warehouse, and I had been working hard. I rolled up the sleeves on my T-shirt and tied a knot in it just above my belly button. When he said it was inappropriate, I rolled down my sleeves and untied the knot. Jerry Black was working next to me, and he told Singleton that he was not offended by the T-shirt. Singleton made some comment that I was at work and not at the beach.

Hamilton had walked past me about fifteen minutes before Singleton, and he did not say anything about my attire. In fact, he smiled at me as he walked by.

A few days later, I wore a loose fitting T-shirt to work. On the front, it said "If you can read this, you're staring." When Black saw it, he made some comment about being a slow reader. Janet Long was working nearby. When she heard his comment, she told Black that his illiteracy finally was paying off. I laughed at her joke, but I did not say anything to either Black or Long.

Later in the morning, Hamilton walked through the warehouse. He looked at my T-shirt and made a comment about reading the fine print. Black made some comment about Hamilton having poor eyesight and needing a closer look. Hamilton laughed at the joke. I laughed at their jokes, but did not make any other comment.

A short time later, Singleton arrived and the trouble started. He told me that the T-shirt was inappropriate and that I had to turn it inside out. Black suggested that I make the change right there, but Singleton did not say anything to him. Singleton told me to reverse the T-shirt on my next break. I do not recall saying anything to Singleton about taking my T-shirt off right there.

My fourth week on the job started uneventfully. I thought that my performance was improving, and Singleton was not spending as much time in my area. However, on Thursday, June 4, YR-2, Singleton was waiting for me when I came to work. I had overslept that morning and could not ride with Lisa. I did not get to the warehouse until 8:10 a.m. That was the first time I had been late since I started at Pinnacle. Singleton told me he was writing me up for being late and my general conduct. The written reprimand mentioned that I was late, that I dressed inappropriately, and that I was a slow worker.

Singleton gave Hamilton a copy of the write-up. Hamilton told me to stop in his office on my next break when he was making his morning rounds. I went to his office just before my lunch break. Hamilton had a copy of the reprimand on his desk and started reading it. He asked me what I had to say, and I told him that I had overslept that morning. Hamilton asked me why my boyfriend had not awakened me. I told him that I did not have a boyfriend and that I was sleeping alone. He again reminded me that I was on probation and that I would not be hired as a permanent employee if I continued to have problems.

Hamilton gave me the write-up to sign before I left his office. I was leaning over the side of the desk to sign my name when he walked around behind me and bumped against me. When I turned to leave, Hamilton was standing between me and the door. He commented that if I did not have a boyfriend he would like to take me out that weekend. I said no and walked past him and out of his office.

I did not want Hamilton to be mad at me because I knew that he would make the final decision on my job. When he was walking through the warehouse that afternoon, I made a point of saying hi to him. He stopped to talk for a minute, but he did not say anything about going out or my job performance.

That Saturday afternoon, I was leaving my apartment to meet some friends and to go shopping. As I started to open the main door to the apartment building, I saw Hamilton driving down the street. I waited a minute to make sure he was gone and walked to my car. As I was pulling my car out of the parking lot, I saw Hamilton again coming from the other direction. I looked in my rearview mirror several times as I was driving down the street, but Hamilton did not turn around or attempt to follow me.

When I returned to work on Monday, June 8, YR-2, Hamilton was walking out of his office. He stopped and said hello and asked whether I had enjoyed the weekend. I told him that I had had a good weekend and asked him what he had done that weekend. He commented that he was not a "swinging single" and that his weekend had been uneventful. Neither one of us commented on him driving past my apartment on Saturday afternoon.

I was concerned about the fact that Hamilton had asked me out and had driven past my apartment. When I saw Singleton, I told him that I was being sexually harassed by Hamilton. Singleton told me it was all my fault because I was flirting with Hamilton. Singleton also asked me, "Do you want to keep your job?" and walked away.

Monday was another hot day in the warehouse. Nothing special happened that morning. After I completed my lunch break, I threw some cold water on my face and neck to cool down. My T-shirt was a little wet when I returned to my work station. Black made a comment to me about joining a wet T-shirt contest, and I asked him whether he thought that I would win. Long heard his comment and told Black that she was going to hose him down with cold water. Black made some comment about holding the hose and judging a wet T-shirt contest between Long and me. After the brief bantering, all three of us returned to work.

As luck would have it, Singleton walked past and saw my T-shirt. He again commented that my appearance was inappropriate. Black made some comment to Singleton about a company wet T-shirt contest that afternoon. Singleton just looked at Black and told him not to encourage me.

Singleton continued to watch me the rest of the week. It seemed that he came around either just before or just after a break to see whether I left early or returned late. Although Singleton sometimes would stop and talk to other employees, he never asked me how things were going or even said good morning.

On Wednesday, June 10, Lisa dropped something on her foot and had to leave the plant to have her foot x-rayed. On my afternoon break, I called a friend, Ron Harper, and asked him to pick me up after work. I left the plant shortly after 4:30 p.m. and walked to the main gate to wait for Harper. Around 5:00 p.m., Hamilton drove up to the main gate and asked me whether I needed a ride. I told him that I was waiting for a friend and did not need a ride. Hamilton asked me whether the friend was male or female, and I told him the friend was someone I worked with at my last job. I did not tell him my friend was a man because I did not think that it was any of his business. Hamilton did not repeat the question, but he continued to make small talk. I got the impression that he was waiting to see who came. A few minutes later, Harper came, and I said goodbye to Hamilton.

On Thursday morning, I drove myself to work because Lisa had a doctor's appointment. Hamilton was standing near the entrance to the warehouse when I got there. He asked me to step into his office and told me that Singleton had complained about the wet T-shirt incident. Hamilton said that Singleton did not have much of a sense of humor at work but that he was a good guy when you got to know him. Hamilton then added that I would find that he also was a great guy if I took the time to get to know him.

When I asked Hamilton whether I could go to my work station, he asked me where I had gone after work. I told him that Harper was only a friend and that he dropped me off at my apartment. Hamilton commented that if I had let him drive me home, he would have treated me to dinner. I thanked him for offering me the ride and went to my work station.

I got to my station around 8:15 a.m., and Singleton was waiting for me. Before he could say anything to me I told him that I had been talking to Hamilton. Singleton made some comment about me trying to keep my job the "old-fashioned way" and walked away. I was offended because Hamilton kept coming on to me, and I had not encouraged him. I started to tell Singleton that Hamilton was making the advances, but he waved his hands and continued to walk away.

On Monday, June 15, YR-2, Hamilton again stopped me as I entered the warehouse. He asked me whether I had a good weekend, and I said yes. He then asked me whether I had seen Harper, and I told him again that we were only friends and not dating. Hamilton also asked me whether I had spent my entire paycheck at the mall. This comment freaked me out, and I wondered how he knew that I had been shopping. I did not say anything to Hamilton about the comment, but I was concerned that he may have been stalking me.

Singleton came up to me as soon as I got to my work station. He told me that he knew that I was not late because he saw me flirting with Hamilton. I told him that I was not flirting with Hamilton and that Hamilton had stopped me on my way into the warehouse. Singleton told me that if I did a better job, I would not have to flirt with Hamilton.

I saw Michelle Johnson, the human resources director, walking through the warehouse. I left the line and walked over to tell her about my problems with Hamilton. Before I could talk to her, I looked back and saw that Singleton was staring at me. I walked past Johnson and got a drink of water before returning to the line. Singleton never took his eyes off me the entire time.

On Thursday, Hamilton stopped me as I was leaving work. He asked me to step into his office, and I did. Hamilton told me that his birthday was Saturday and asked me whether I wanted to go out and celebrate with him. I told him that I did not think it was a good idea for me to date the boss and declined his invitation. Hamilton was standing between me and the door, and I felt uncomfortable. I told him that I had to leave and walked past him.

Lisa had been off work all week because of her injured foot. On Friday, I had car problems and had to call the garage for a jump. When I arrived at work around 8:20, Singleton was waiting for me. I told him that I had car problems and that I had a receipt to prove it. Singleton told me that he was going to give me another written reprimand.

Hamilton walked through the warehouse several times on Friday and never looked at me. I felt like I was in trouble because Singleton was going to give me another write-up and Hamilton was ignoring me. As I left work on Friday, I stopped in Hamilton's office. I wished him a happy birthday and said that I hoped he had a nice weekend. He asked me whether I had changed my mind about dinner on Saturday, and I told him that I had not.

On Monday, June 22, YR-2, I rode to work with Lisa for the first time since her injury. I asked her to leave early because I did not want to be late. When I walked into the warehouse at 7:50 a.m., I did not see Singleton or Hamilton and went directly to my work station.

Long arrived a few minutes later and told me that she saw Singleton and Hamilton at the employees' entrance to the warehouse. She said that they were not really talking to each other, and it appeared as though they were looking for someone. I knew that that was not a good sign. Black came to the work area about ten minutes later. He commented on being a few minutes late and having to walk past Hamilton and Singleton. He said he just smiled and kept walking as fast as he could.

I was working around 8:15 a.m. when I saw Singleton coming in my direction. I continued to work and tried to ignore him, but he came up to me with another write-up in his hand. The first thing he said to me was "How did you sneak in?" I told him that I had punched in before 8:00 a.m. and that he could check my time card if he did not believe me. Singleton then told me that he had "another present" for me and handed me the reprimand. It stated I had been late for work on Friday and included the same complaints of being a slow worker and taking longer breaks than I was allowed. Singleton told me that Hamilton wanted to see me immediately.

I went to Hamilton's office, and he was waiting for me with a copy of the write-up. He told me that Singleton had been complaining about me from the start and that he had tried to convince Singleton to give me time to adjust to the new job. Hamilton said that it did not appear as though I had a future with the company and that I should punch out and turn in my ID badge.

I was upset because I was doing my best, and I asked Hamilton to give me some more time to work things out. I told him that I had come in early because I was late on Friday and had not wanted to be late again. Hamilton told me that I was not entitled to any more chances and that his mind was made up.

I told Hamilton that I was being fired because I would not go out with him. He just said that I had missed out on another opportunity. Hamilton then called security, and I was escorted out of the plant.

It took me two weeks to find another job as a cashier at the Mega Mart. That job only paid me $8.50 per hour for the first six months and $9.00 per hour for the next six months. After one year, I was appointed assistant manager and received a salary of $19,500 per year.

When I was hired at Pinnacle Packaging Products, I received a copy of the Employee Handbook. I am aware that the handbook prohibits harassment and provides for reporting any incidents to the Human Resources Department. The administrative offices are in another building next to the warehouse, and I went to the Human Resources Department to complete the paperwork when I was hired. I never filed a complaint with Human Resources about Hamilton either before or after I was fired. I attempted to complain to Michelle Johnson on one occasion, but Singleton was watching me. When I had complained to him, Singleton threatened to fire me. I did not want to lose my job, so I continued to work and hoped that Hamilton would get the message.

As you asked, I checked my diary and brought you copies of the entries that have to do with Hamilton. They are what you are now showing me, Exhibit T-1. I also recall sending an email to Lisa on May 26, YR-2, stating my concerns about Hamilton. Lisa might have kept a copy.

I certify that the above is a true and accurate transcript of the deposition of Jamie Taylor taken this 11th day of August, YR-1.

Jamie Taylor

DJ Sullivan

D.J. Sullivan
Certified Court Reporter

Excerpts from Taylor's Diary

May 11, YR-2   Started work today at Pinnacle. Seems OK place.

May 15, YR-2   H putting the moves on me—not gonna put up with any crap.

May 25, YR-2   H & S trying to fake up reasons to fire me—BS discip report.

DEPOSITION OF LISA ROBERTS

My name is Lisa Roberts, and I was employed by Pinnacle Packaging Products from June YR-6 until I was terminated in May of YR-1. I worked on one of the packaging lines supervised by Chuck Singleton. John Hamilton was the warehouse manager, and Singleton reported directly to him.

I was terminated by Pinnacle after Jamie Taylor, the plaintiff in this lawsuit, filed her case against Pinnacle. In February YR-1, Jamie's lawyer asked me if I would be willing to be a witness in the case for Jamie and tell what I knew about Jamie's troubles at the company and about rumors about Hamilton's behavior to female employees. I said I would tell anything and everything I knew. I guess that news got around the plant, because in April Hamilton and Singleton called me into Hamilton's office and asked me if I was going to be a witness for Jamie. I pretended not to know anything about the lawsuit because I was afraid of what would happen to me, so I said I didn't know anything about it and I was not "planning" to be a witness. But a few weeks later, toward the end of April, Singleton started to write me up for every little thing—taking a long break, being a few minutes late in the morning, and a violation of a supposed "dress code." Then, in early May, they terminated me for "repeated lateness." I think they fired me because they were mad about me agreeing to be a witness for Jamie, which I'm sure they had a way to find out. Since then, I have been on unemployment benefits—but that's hardly enough to live on, so I have had to use all my savings just to make ends meet.

Singleton supervised the packaging lines that are adjacent to each other. If I was at my work station, I could not see what was happening on the other line. Singleton was my immediate supervisor the entire time I worked at Pinnacle.

In April YR-2, I heard that there was an opening on the other packaging line. Jamie Taylor and I have been friends since high school, and I knew that she was looking for a new job. I talked to Hamilton about Jamie, and he told me to tell Jamie to fill out a job application.

Jamie completed the application, and I brought it to work and gave it to Hamilton. A few days later, Jamie told me that she had a job interview with Hamilton. The front of Hamilton's office is mostly windows, and I could see Jamie and Hamilton talking. A short time later, I saw Hamilton showing Jamie around the warehouse.

I was returning from my lunch break when Hamilton came up to me and told me that he had hired Jamie. I thanked him for hiring her, and he said that I should tell all my other good-looking friends to apply for a job.

Jamie started working on Monday, May 11, YR-2, and I drove her to work because we were on the same shift. Jamie did not have any problems the first week, but she did say that it was hard work.

At the end of the week, we decided to go to Kool's Korner to celebrate Singleton's birthday. I drove Jamie to Kool's and called my boyfriend and told him to meet us there after work. The bar was crowded, and we all were standing around having a drink or two. Some of the people started to leave, and so we got a few tables to push together so we could sit down. My boyfriend had arrived, and he sat on one side of me and Jamie sat on the other side.

Hamilton was not there at first, and after I sat down I saw him for the first time. Hamilton sat next to Jamie, and Singleton was sitting across from Hamilton. After we got seated, Hamilton bought a round of drinks for everyone.

I spent most of my time talking to my boyfriend and the people across from us. Occasionally, I said something to Jamie, but she spent most of her time talking to Hamilton and Singleton. We may have been seated about an hour when Jamie moved closer to me. At first I did not think anything of it, but a short time later she moved closer again. Before I could say anything to her, Jamie said she needed more room and glanced at Hamilton. I could see that he was getting close to Jamie, so I moved over to give her more room.

A few minutes later, Jamie asked me when I was leaving. I had just gotten another drink, and I told her I would give her a ride home when I finished it. I do not know what Jamie and Hamilton said to each other, but about ten minutes later, Jamie told me that she was leaving and Hamilton was driving her home. I was having a good time, so I was pleased that I did not have to leave.

About thirty minutes after they left, Jamie called me on my cell phone. I had had about four or five drinks by then, and the bar was noisy. Jamie made some comment to me about Hamilton kissing her good night. I told her that Hamilton was not the worst guy she had kissed, and she commented that he was the oldest. Our conversation was short, but I did not feel that Jamie was upset.

I did not talk to Jamie until I picked her up for work on Monday. I told Jamie that she would be hired permanently for sure if she started dating Hamilton. Jamie told me that she had no intention of going out with Hamilton and that they both had been drinking when they kissed. She did not seem upset about the incident, but I could tell that she did not want to be teased about it.

Jamie and I saw Hamilton in his office with Singleton when we walked into the warehouse. Jamie went directly to her work station, and I went to mine. I cannot see the other line from where I work, so I do not know what happened that day. Jamie did not say anything about either Hamilton or Singleton on our way home that evening.

Hamilton generally walked through the warehouse several times a day. At times, he would stop and talk to someone. Because Singleton was responsible for the two packaging lines, he could not watch us all the time. I saw him in Hamilton's office many times, and he made calls to other parts of the plant to check on production and shipping.

We were entitled to two fifteen-minute breaks during the day and a thirty-minute lunch break. We could not take the breaks at the same time because we had to keep the line moving. We did not have to punch a time clock when we took a break. Sometimes I would see Jamie when I had a break. I know Jamie did not always get back to her work station on time. A few times she would stay with me if I went into the break room when she already was there. I also saw Jamie talking to other workers at times as she was returning to her job. Everyone took a few extra minutes some days, and Jamie was no different than anyone else.

I was not aware that Jamie was having any problems with Singleton until later in the week. Jamie complained that Singleton was watching her all the time and criticizing her work. I had not had any problems with Singleton, and I encouraged Jamie to hang in there and do her best.

If someone got a written reprimand, he had to meet with Hamilton and Singleton. The employee had to sign the reprimand, and there is a place for the employee to write in any comments. I believe the reprimand then is put in the employee's file. The following Monday, I heard through the gossip mill that Jamie had received a write-up and was seen in Hamilton's office. After work, Jamie told me that she had received the reprimand and had met with Singleton and Hamilton. After Singleton left, Jamie said that Hamilton asked her out and reminded her that he had the final decision on her future with the company.

One day, Jamie was wearing a T-shirt that said, "If you can read this, you're staring." I told her that the shirt would get her some attention, and she laughed. I was not aware that Singleton had complained about the rolled up T-shirt. If I had heard about that, I may have said something to Jamie about her latest T-shirt. When Jamie met me after work, the T-shirt was inside out. Jamie told me that Singleton had made her reverse the shirt on one of her breaks.

On June 4, YR-2, Jamie called me as I was getting ready to leave my apartment. She told me that she had overslept and that she would drive herself to work. I do not know what time she got to work, but later I saw Jamie, and she told me that she had received another reprimand from Singleton.

Jamie also complained about her meeting with Hamilton. Apparently, Hamilton had made some comment about sleeping with her boyfriend and brushed against her when she was leaning over the desk to sign the write-up. Jamie also said that Hamilton had asked her out again but that she would not go out with him even if it meant losing her job.

On June 10, YR-2, I dropped a box on my foot and had to leave the plant to have it x-rayed. Before I left, I told Jamie that she would have to find a ride home.

A few days before my accident, Jamie had another run-in with Singleton. It was a hot day, and I saw Jamie as she was leaving the break room after lunch. Her hair was wet and so was her T-shirt. I did not say anything to her, but I was not surprised when she later told me that Singleton had complained about her wet T-shirt. Jamie also laughed and said that if Hamilton had walked past her, the wet T-shirt would have guaranteed her a permanent job.

I was off work until Monday, June 22, YR-2. I had talked to Jamie several times while I was off, but she did not say anything about either Singleton or Hamilton. However, when she called me Sunday to confirm that I would give her a ride to work, she asked if we could leave early because she did not want to be late. I told her that I had to go to the Human Resources Department before I could start working and that leaving early was a good idea. We got to the plant about twenty minutes early, and Jamie went directly to the warehouse. I know that she started work before 8:00 a.m.

Later that day, I heard that Jamie had been fired. I know some other probationary workers had not been hired full time, but this was the first time I saw someone fired before the end of the sixty-day period.

I called Jamie later that day when I got home. Jamie said that she had told Hamilton she was fired because she had not gone out with him. Jamie said Hamilton made some comment about missing out on two good opportunities.

I did once go to HR a few months before Jamie was hired and told Michelle Johnson that I was having a problem with Hamilton sexually harassing me, but it was really just BS. I thought his behavior was a little weird, but nothing out of the ordinary when you're working around a bunch of guys. I only complained because I wanted to be on record in case something happened later that I really didn't like.

As you asked, I checked my diary and found nothing in there about Jamie or Hamilton. I did find one email from Jamie about Hamilton, Exhibit R-1.

I certify that the above is a true and accurate transcript of the deposition of Lisa Roberts taken this 18th day of August, YR-1.

Lisa Roberts
_____

D.J. Sullivan
_____

D.J. Sullivan
Certified Court Reporter

Taylor's Email to Roberts

From: jtaylor@aol.nita

To: lisarob@mindspring.nita

Re: work idea

Date: May 26, YR-2

You know how I told you Hamilton has put a few moves on me at work, after that first time at the bar my first week? It's not too bad—we're used to that sort of thing, aren't we, from guys at work—but I'm not going to let it go if it gets worse. Plus, they're starting to hassle me now about working slow and taking long breaks. Do you think I have to start reporting him every time he gets physical?

DEPOSITION OF JERRY BLACK

My name is Jerry Black, and I have worked at Pinnacle Packaging Products since June YR-6. Sometime in May YR-2, Jamie Taylor was hired by the company and assigned to my packaging line. John Hamilton is the warehouse manager, and Chuck Singleton is the foreman of my line and another line located nearby.

I am not good at remembering dates, but shortly after Jamie started we went out for drinks at Kool's Korner to celebrate Singleton's birthday. We were all standing around because the bar was crowded and there was no place for all of us to sit. I remember talking to Jamie briefly that evening, but I only stayed for one drink. I do not remember whether Hamilton got there before I left, but some of the employees were pushing tables together so they could sit down. I left before people got seated. On Monday, I did not hear any gossip about what may have happened after I left.

I have seen a number of people come and go from my packaging line. It can be hard work because you have to keep busy and lift some heavy boxes. Jamie is an average-sized woman and had problems lifting some heavy boxes. She appeared to work hard and catch on to the program. I was not watching her all the time, and we were not partners. However, she was doing a good job, especially for a new employee.

Jamie is very friendly and talked to anyone who was in the area. She also was attractive and somewhat of a tease. The warehouse is not air conditioned and can get hot in the summer. One day, Jamie rolled up the sleeves on her T-shirt and tied the bottom of her T-shirt showing off some of her belly. Of course, the guys on the line approved of her appearance and some comments were made. Jamie responded to some of the comments and seemed to enjoy the attention. A short time later, Singleton came to the line and told Jamie to untie the knot in her T-shirt. Jamie did what she was told, and some of the guys made a few comments to Singleton about spoiling the fun.

About one week later, Jamie wore a T-shirt that said "If you can read this, you're staring." Several comments were made by some of the guys. I made a comment about being a slow reader, and Janet Long said something about me being illiterate. Hamilton saw the T-shirt when he walked by. I could not hear what he and Jamie said, but they were laughing. Jamie seemed to enjoy the banter until Singleton showed up and complained about the T-shirt. He told her to turn the shirt inside out on her next break. Jamie said, "You want me to turn it inside out right here—I don't mind." All the guys started to cheer, but Singleton didn't seem amused.

One or two weeks later, Singleton was upset with Jamie after she returned from lunch. It was another hot day in the warehouse, and Jamie had put her head under the faucet or something to cool off. Her hair and T-shirt were wet when she returned to the work area. Of course, some of the other guys and I noticed and made some comments. I believe I suggested a company wet T-shirt contest. Jamie and Janet made some comments back to us, and I thought the incident was over. However, Singleton walked up and was noticeably upset by Jamie's appearance.

For some reason, Singleton seemed to have it in for Jamie almost from the start. We are entitled to a fifteen-minute break in the morning, another fifteen-minute break in the afternoon, and thirty minutes for lunch. We do not have to punch a time clock for our breaks, and sometimes someone gets back a little late. Singleton seemed to be watching Jamie and noticed when she was not back to work on time or stopped to talk to someone while she was walking back to the line.

Jamie never said anything to me about Hamilton. Whenever Hamilton walked through the warehouse, Jamie made a point to talk to him. Their conversations were not long, and most of the time I could not hear what they were saying. I considered Jamie a flirt, and she acted that way with Hamilton.

I am aware that Jamie received some write-ups from Singleton and that she was called into Hamilton's office several times because of it. She never told me any details, but she did say that Singleton was picking on her. I was surprised when Jamie was fired before her probationary period ended. I know of some people who were not hired full time after sixty days, but I am not aware of anyone who was not allowed to complete the probationary period. I thought that Jamie was trying hard and doing the best that she could. Some probationary employees who did not work as hard as Jamie were allowed to complete the sixty-day period before they were fired.

I certify that the above is a true and accurate transcript of the deposition of Jerry Black taken this 18th day of August, YR-1.

Jerry Black
_____

D.J. Sullivan
_____

D.J. Sullivan
Certified Court Reporter

DEPOSITION OF JOHN HAMILTON

My name is John Hamilton, and my date of birth is June 26, YR-44. In February YR-2, my wife Nancy and I separated. A few weeks later, Nancy filed for divorce and got a restraining order against me. Shortly after we separated, I was at our house and Nancy and I had an argument. Both of us were yelling, and I got mad and knocked over a lamp. I never hit Nancy or threw anything at her, but her lawyer asked the judge for a restraining order. I realized we would not reconcile, so I did not contest the restraining order. I never violated that order. Our divorce became final August 18, YR-2.

I have worked for Pinnacle Packaging Products since September YR-21. In January YR-16, I became the foreman for two packaging lines. Chuck Singleton worked for me and became foreman when I was promoted to warehouse manager in October YR-12.

Lisa Roberts used to work on one of the packaging lines supervised by Singleton until she was fired for poor performance in YR-1. When an opening on the line occurred in April YR-2, Lisa mentioned that she had a friend, Jamie Taylor, who was looking for a job. Lisa had been doing a good job, so I was willing to accept her recommendation. I told Lisa to have her friend fill out an employment application from the Human Resources Department. By the way, that should take care of any idea that I held a grudge against Lisa for a complaint she had filed against me a few months before this.

Jamie Taylor came in for a job interview in May YR-2, and I offered her a job. Jamie accepted and agreed to start on Monday, May 11, YR-2. I sent her to the Human Resources Department to talk to Michelle Johnson and complete the paperwork.

All new employees are hired for a sixty-day probationary period. After the sixty days, they become permanent employees and receive health insurance and other benefits. I explained this to Jamie, and it also is covered in the Employee Handbook that each new employee receives.

I walk through the warehouse several times a day to see how things are going. I know all of the employees by name, and I greet them or talk to them briefly, especially if they are on a break. When I was walking through the warehouse after I had offered Jamie the job, I stopped to talk to Lisa. I told Lisa that I had hired Jamie and thanked her for recommending her. I know that Lisa has said that I made a comment about hiring all of her good-looking friends. I may have made a joke like that, but I do not remember what was said.

Jamie was assigned to one of the lines supervised by Singleton. Jamie and Lisa did not work on the same line, and you cannot see what is going on at the other line from your work station. Some of the employees talk on breaks even though they work on different lines.

Singleton is responsible for supervising the lines and dealing with any problems that might come up. If a problem is serious enough, the employee will receive a written reprimand. I will review the write-up with the employee. Most of the time Singleton or the supervisor who handed out the reprimand will attend the meeting. The employee is required to sign the write-up and can make any comments if there is a dispute about what occurred.

I have the final say on who is hired or fired in the warehouse. Although I do watch what is happening in the warehouse, normally I rely on the recommendation of my foremen when I make the final decision.

I do not remember anything out of the ordinary during Jamie's first week on the job. I saw her working several times, and she seemed to be learning the job. During the first week, a new employee is assigned to someone for training, so Jamie had someone helping her do the work. I did notice that Jamie had problems lifting some of the heavier packages.

Occasionally, Jamie and I would exchange greetings when I was in that area. During the first week, I only talked to her two or three times to ask her how things were going. Jamie never had any complaints about the work or about Singleton.

On May 15, YR-2, some employees decided to stop for drinks after work to celebrate Singleton's birthday. They told me they were going to Kool's Korner, and I said that I would meet them when I finished a few things in the warehouse. I left work about one hour after everyone else.

When I got to Kool's Korner, some of the employees already had left. Lisa and some other people were pushing tables together so everyone could sit down. I talked to Singleton while they were doing this and then sat down across the table from him. When I sat down, I noticed that Jamie was sitting on my right and Lisa was sitting next to her. A young man was sitting on the other side of Lisa, and Jamie said that he was Lisa's boyfriend.

Lisa was spending a lot of time talking to her boyfriend, so Jamie talked to Singleton and me quite a bit. I do not know how many drinks Jamie had before I got there, but I did buy one round for the table. Jamie was very friendly, and I did not see anything to suggest that she and Singleton were having any problems at work.

Jamie was sitting close to me at the table and frequently rubbed or bumped against me. After about one hour, I put my hand on her knee. Jamie did not say anything or pull away, so I left it there for a minute or two. Jamie was wearing jeans just like everyone else at work.

I could tell that Lisa was having a good time and was not planning on leaving soon. I heard Jamie ask Lisa when she was leaving, and Lisa said that she wanted to finish her drink. I was not planning on staying much longer, so I offered to give Jamie a ride home. She accepted my offer without any hesitation.

Jamie lives in an apartment building on Main Street in Nita City, and it took me about five or ten minutes to drive there. I stopped in front of her apartment building, and we talked for a few more minutes. I do not remember what we were talking about, but she seemed very relaxed and not in a hurry to get out of the car. I leaned over and kissed her. Jamie did not pull away or resist. After we kissed, Jamie said good night and got out of the car. She did not seem upset by the fact that I kissed her.

After Jamie left, I realized that kissing her was not a good idea because I was her boss and there was a significant age difference between us. I was not going to say anything about it to Jamie on Monday and see how she reacted.

I saw Jamie Monday, May 18, YR-2, when I was walking through the warehouse. We exchanged greetings, and neither one of us said anything about what happened Friday evening. I did not tell Singleton or anyone else about the incident.

Some time that week, around the middle of the week, I think, Singleton told me that he was not satisfied with Jamie's performance. He said that she was a slow worker and did not return to the line promptly when her break was over. I told Singleton to let me know if the problems continued.

When I walked through the warehouse during that week, I made an effort to watch Jamie and see whether her performance was improving. Jamie was very friendly, and I frequently saw her talking to other workers, especially when she was walking to or from a break. She still had problems lifting heavy objects, but I expected her to improve as she got stronger and learned the job. Because of Singleton's concerns I wanted to check her work, so I had Singleton move her work station to in front of my office window—yes, that is accurately shown on Exhibit 11. The move had nothing to do with the events at Kool's or on the drive to Jamie's apartment.

On Thursday, Singleton told me that he was going to issue Jamie a written reprimand if her work did not improve on Friday. I told him that it was his decision to make and that I would talk to him and Jamie Monday morning if he gave her a write-up. Before Singleton left Friday evening, he told me he was going to give Jamie a write-up when she came to work on Monday.

Jamie and Singleton were in my office when I got to work Monday morning. Singleton gave me a copy of the write-up, and I read it quickly. I reminded Jamie that she was on probation and that she might not become a full-time employee if she got any more reprimands.

An employee is required to sign any reprimand before it is sent to the Human Resources Department. Singleton started to leave, and Jamie followed him without signing the reprimand. I told Jamie that she had to sign it, and she stayed in my office after Singleton left. I could see that Jamie was upset, so I offered her some encouragement. I told her the job would get easier as she gained more experience. As she was leaving my office, I told her she was prettier when she smiled. Jamie said that she did not feel like smiling.

I know that Jamie has said that I asked her out for a drink before she left the office. I did not ask her out because we had just discussed her performance and asking her out would not have been appropriate. Jamie left my office immediately after I told her to smile. I talked to Jamie briefly later that day, and she did not appear to be upset with me about anything.

Jamie was involved in another incident with Singleton a few days later. It was hot in the warehouse, and Jamie had rolled up the sleeves on her T-shirt and had tied a knot in the end of the shirt. I saw Jamie but did not say anything to her about her attire. I later learned that Singleton had told her to untie her T-shirt when he walked past a few minutes later.

The following week Jamie had another run-in with Singleton about her attire. She was wearing a T-shirt that said "If you can read this, you're staring." I saw the T-shirt and said I would try to read the fine print. Jerry Black was nearby and heard my comment and said something about stepping closer because I had poor eyesight. Jamie laughed at the jokes and obviously enjoyed the attention. I was not around when Singleton came, but the next time I saw Jamie she was wearing the T-shirt inside out.

I did not notice anything unusual about Jamie's performance as I walked through the warehouse. She frequently greeted me or stopped working for a short time to ask me a question. I knew that Jamie would not be one of our best workers, but she appeared to be making some progress.

Jamie came to work late on June 4, YR-2, and Singleton gave her another write-up. The reprimand also mentioned her general performance and her clothing incidents. I told Jamie to come to my office on her next break, and she stopped in just before lunch. Jamie told me that she had overslept, and I made a comment about her boyfriend waking her up. I intended it as a joke, but I could tell that she was not in a joking mood, so I dropped the boyfriend subject.

I admonished Jamie to work harder and reminded her that she would not be hired as a permanent employee if her performance did not improve. I placed the write-up on my desk for Jamie to sign and left the office for lunch.

My desk is against the wall, and I had to walk behind Jamie to leave my office. I never touched her as I walked past her and did not ask her out for dinner. Later that afternoon, Jamie smiled at me and said hello as I walked through the warehouse. She definitely did not act like she was upset with me.

Jamie's apartment building is on Main Street, which is a heavily traveled highway. I have driven past that apartment building many times both before and after I found out Jamie lived there. I am aware that Jamie claims that she saw me drive past her building and return from the opposite direction a short time later. She may have seen me drive past, but I was not stalking her and did not drive back and forth in front of her apartment. I drive down Main Street any time I drive through town.

I am aware that Singleton was upset with Jamie about the wet T-shirt incident. I did not walk through the warehouse at that time, so I did not see anything. I understand that Jamie encouraged some comments from some of the male workers when they saw her.

On June 10, YR-2, Lisa dropped something on her foot and had to leave the plant for x-rays. Jamie and Lisa rode to work together, and I saw Jamie standing at the main gate when I was leaving work that evening. I asked Jamie if she needed a ride, and she told me that a friend was coming to pick her up. I waited a few minutes to make sure that Jamie had a ride home. We talked as we waited, and then a guy drove up. I asked Jamie if he was her boyfriend, and she said it was just someone she had worked with.

I saw Jamie when she was coming into work the next day. Singleton had complained to me about the wet T-shirt incident, so I mentioned it to Jamie as she walked into the warehouse. I asked her if she needed a ride home that evening, and she said that she had driven herself to work. I told Jamie that she should let me know if she needed a ride while Lisa was off work. I did not really ask her out to dinner, but I made a comment about buying her a McDonald's Happy Meal on the way home. Jamie thanked me and went to her work station. I never asked her any questions about what she and her friend had done the previous evening. I saw Jamie in the warehouse several times that day, and she smiled and greeted me each time. She did not seem to be offended by my offer to give her a ride home.

It was not unusual for me to talk to Jamie either in the warehouse or the break room. I do not remember the specifics of any conversation we may have had on Monday, June 15, YR-2. I am sure that I asked her whether she had a good weekend. I did not ask her about whether she had dated anyone that weekend. Because the previous Friday was payday, I remember asking her if she had spent her paycheck shopping. I have no idea whether she had gone shopping, but I assumed that she had and made the joke.

Nothing eventful occurred between Jamie and me the rest of the week. Either Thursday or Friday, I was talking to Jamie as she was leaving the break room. She asked me if I had any plans for the weekend, and I told her my birthday was on Sunday. I also told Jamie some friends were taking me out to dinner on Saturday. I never asked Jamie to join us. As Jamie left work on Friday, she stopped in my office and wished me a happy birthday. I thanked her and told her to have a nice weekend.

After Jamie left the warehouse, Singleton stopped in my office and told me that Jamie was late for work again that morning. He also said that Jamie was not improving and that he thought she should be fired. We discussed her work record, and I told Singleton that I would send Jamie home when she came to work on Monday. Singleton prepared the write-up and said he would give it to Jamie on Monday.

On Monday, June 22, YR-2, Jamie came into my office after her shift had started. I told her that things were not working out and that Singleton constantly was complaining about her job performance. I told Jamie that she was fired and called security to escort her from the building.

For the first time, Jamie said that she was being fired because she would not go out with me. I told her she knew that was not true and that she had received several warnings. I told her that Lisa had gotten her the job and that she had not taken advantage of the opportunity.

Jamie is the only probationary employee who was not given the full sixty-day probationary period. Singleton told me that Jamie was not improving, and we did not believe anything would change in the remaining few weeks.

A few weeks later, Michelle Johnson told me that Jamie had filed an EEOC charge against the company. I answered her questions during her investigation of the complaint. I never expected things to go this far. When Jamie complained that she was fired for not going out with me, I assumed that she made those comments because she was upset and that nothing would happen when she settled down.

You have the work-log entries I brought with me for this interview today, H-1—those are the only ones that look to me like they have to do with Taylor. The exclamation points after her name are my indication that I thought she was going to be a really good employee. They are not a comment on her appearance.

You also have the email I brought today, H-2—it's the only one I found that concerned Taylor.

I certify that the above is a true and accurate transcript of the deposition of John Hamilton taken this 17th day of August, YR-1.

John Hamilton
_____

D.J. Sullivan
_____
D.J. Sullivan
Certified Court Reporter

Hamilton's Work Log

5/11/YR-2   New employee Taylor (!!!)

5/20/YR-2   Singleton directive: watch employees' break use closely—some are abusing?

6/15–19/YR-2   Watching Roberts and Taylor esp, due to potential break abuse

6/22/YR-2   Terminated Taylor for poor work habits, inappropriate dress. She claims that it was because she wouldn't go out with me. I told her that was not true.

Hamilton's Email to Singleton

From: Hamilton@pinnacle.nita

To: singleton@pinnacle.nita

Re: New hire Taylor

Date: May 18, YR-2

I have some concerns about the work habits of new hire Taylor—on-time arrival, too many breaks, dress code. What do you advise?

DEPOSITION OF CHUCK SINGLETON

My name is Chuck Singleton, and I have worked at Pinnacle Packaging Products for sixteen years. When John Hamilton became warehouse manager nine years ago, I replaced him as the foreman on two packaging lines. Lisa Roberts worked on one of my lines for about four years, until she was terminated in YR-1 for poor performance.

When an opening occurred on the line, Lisa told me that she had a friend who was looking for a job. I told Lisa that she would have to talk to Hamilton because he made all of the hiring and firing decisions. A few weeks later, Jamie Taylor was hired.

All new employees are on probation for sixty days. Working on the packaging line can be hard work because you have to work quickly and lift some heavy packages. From the beginning, I had doubts whether Jamie would be able to handle the job.

During the first week, Jamie was being trained and frequently worked with another employee or me. I noticed that Jamie liked to talk and should have spent more time working. When she started working by herself the second week, she was not getting things done quickly enough. I started to make comments to Jamie to prod her to work faster.

Every employee is entitled to a fifteen-minute break in the morning and in the afternoon plus thirty minutes for lunch. The line never shuts down, so the employees are expected to take their breaks when things slow down or when someone can cover. We do not require employees to punch in and out for breaks. If someone starts abusing the break times, I will say something.

Jamie had problems with the breaks almost from the start. Sometimes she would talk to other employees as they started or ended their breaks. Employees also may leave for quick bathroom breaks at times. Jamie seemed to think that she should not have to use her scheduled breaks to go to the bathroom.

At the end of Jamie's first week on the job, we went to Kool's Korner to celebrate my birthday. Jamie arrived with Lisa and left with Hamilton. We were seated at a table for one or two hours before they left. I did not see any touching between Hamilton and Jamie while they were at Kool's. Jamie did not seem reluctant to leave with Hamilton.

The next Monday, Hamilton instructed me to move Jamie's work station to in front of his office window—so he could "keep an eye on her," were his words. I assumed he meant he wanted to check on her work, but he did kind of laugh when he said it—sort of a chuckle, if you know what I mean.

After Jamie was fired, I heard some allegations about Hamilton harassing her. Hamilton never told me that he asked Jamie out and never said anything to me about how I was treating her. I saw Hamilton and Jamie talking many times when he was walking through the warehouse. Since Jamie was somewhat of a flirt, I just assumed she was trying to curry favor with the boss.

I gave Jamie her first written reprimand on May 25, YR-2. It was because she was not working quickly enough and was spending too much time away from her work station. If I give someone a write-up, the employee and I then meet with Hamilton to discuss the problem.

Our meeting with Hamilton was uneventful. He told Jamie that she would have to do a better job if she wanted to become a permanent employee after the probationary period. An employee must sign any reprimand and can add any comments. I left Hamilton's office when Jamie was signing the reprimand. Neither Hamilton nor Jamie said anything to me about any conversations that they may have had after I left his office.

Later that week, I verbally reprimanded Jamie for her appearance. It was hot in the warehouse, and Jamie had rolled up the sleeves on her T-shirt and had tied up the bottom of the T-shirt so her belly was showing. I told her that her appearance was inappropriate and to untie the knot and roll the T-shirt down. Jerry Black made some comment about how good Jamie looked, but I told him we were not at the beach.

A few days later, Jamie wore a T-shirt that said, "If you can read this, you're staring." I told Jamie that she should not wear a T-shirt like that to work and to reverse it on her next break. Black again made some comment about making Jamie change the shirt immediately. Jamie was amused, but I was not.

Jamie's performance never changed significantly over the next week or so. Sometimes she worked harder, but I felt that she worked harder only when I was around. On June 4, YR-2, Jamie was late for work. I gave her another write-up for being late, her overall job performance, and her inappropriate clothes.

I gave Hamilton a copy of the second reprimand, and he said that he would talk to Jamie. Things were busy that morning, and I did not attend the meeting between Jamie and Hamilton. I do not know what was said at the meeting, but later in the afternoon I saw Jamie approach Hamilton as he walked through the plant. They spoke for a minute or two before he continued his rounds.

I had another problem with Jamie the following Monday. It was another hot day in the warehouse, and Jamie must have poured water over her head during her lunch break. When I saw her at her work station, her hair and T-shirt were all wet. I told Jamie that her appearance was not appropriate, and Black again had to make some comment. I could tell that Jamie enjoyed the attention she was getting.

On Friday, June 19, YR-2, Jamie again was late for work. When I confronted her, she said that she had car problems. This was the second time that she had been late, and her overall performance had not improved. Rather than giving her another write-up, I decided to talk to Hamilton directly about the problem.

Friday was a busy day, and I did not have a chance to talk to Hamilton until after the employees had left. I told him that Jamie had been late again and that her overall performance had not improved. We discussed all of the problems, and Hamilton said that he would send Jamie home when she came to work on Monday.

I prepared the final write-up and planned on giving it to Jamie when she came to work on Monday, June 22, YR-2. I did not see her come in, and I found her at the work station around 8:15 a.m. I gave her the reprimand and told Jamie that she had to see Hamilton immediately. I did not go to Hamilton's office, but later I saw security escorting Jamie out of the warehouse.

A few weeks after Jamie was fired, Michelle Johnson from the Human Resources Department contacted me. She told me that Jamie had filed an EEOC charge and claimed sexual harassment by Hamilton. I told Michelle that Hamilton never said anything to me about asking Jamie out and that all of the complaints about Jamie's performance came from me and not Hamilton. Although Hamilton has the final say, I was the one who recommended that Jamie get fired. Jamie's complaint sounds to me like something she and Lisa Roberts cooked up together, since Lisa had filed a similar one against Hamilton shortly before Jamie was hired. I'll bet Lisa is going to turn up as a witness for Jamie in this case.

To my knowledge, Jamie is the only probationary employee who was fired before the sixty-day period ended. I saw no reason to delay the decision because her performance was not improving.

I am aware that Jamie has claimed that she complained to me about Hamilton and that I threatened to fire her. That never happened. However, I told her on more than one occasion to stop flirting and start working if she wanted to keep her job.

I certify that the above is a true and accurate transcript of the deposition of Chuck Singleton taken this 18th day of August, YR-1.

C Singleton

_____

DJ Sullivan

_____

D.J. Sullivan
Certified Court Reporter

Deposition of Michelle Johnson

My name is Michelle Johnson, and I have been the Human Resources Director for Pinnacle Packaging Products since January YR-8. Part of my duties includes processing the paperwork for employees who are joining or leaving the company. I also am responsible for implementing our EEOC (Equal Employment Opportunity Commission) program. It is against company policy to discriminate against any employee because of race, gender, or national origin. This policy also forbids any form of harassment. Exhibit 5 is a copy of that policy.

Each new employee receives an Employee Handbook, which explains our EEOC policy and how to report any violations. Employees are encouraged, but not required, to report any problems to their immediate supervisor. The handbook also tells employees that they may file a complaint directly with the Human Resources Department. Exhibit 5 contains that information.

My office is in the administration building adjacent to the warehouse. All new employees come to the Human Resources Department when they are hired to complete the required paperwork. Employees also come to my office if they have any questions about their paychecks or fringe benefits. Every employee knows where the Human Resources office is located.

The warehouse has fewer than fifty employees, and the work force is fairly stable. I know all of the employees on a first name basis. I do not go to the warehouse every day, but I always talk to employees if I see any of them in the break room.

I completed the paperwork for Jamie Taylor when she was hired and gave her a copy of the Employee Handbook. On more than one occasion, I saw Jamie when I was in the warehouse. Jamie never said anything to me about any sexual harassment claims involving John Hamilton. She never filed any formal complaints with the Human Resources office before she was fired.

I also am in charge of maintaining the employee personnel files. If an employee receives a written reprimand or any other disciplinary action, I receive a copy and place it in the employee's file. I am not notified if the employee only receives a verbal warning or reprimand. If the employee disagrees with a write-up, the employee can put a comment on the written reprimand.

I am not responsible for investigating any disputes over reprimands unless they involve a potential violation of the company EEOC policy. If Jamie had commented on any of her reprimands that Hamilton was harassing her because she would not go out with him, I would have conducted an investigation.

Jamie was making $9.50 per hour when she was fired. If she had completed her sixty-day probationary period, she also would have received medical insurance. After six months as a permanent employee, Jamie would have received a $.50-an-hour raise. One year later, Jamie would have received another $.50-an-hour pay raise.

I was not aware of any problem between Hamilton and Jamie until I received a copy of the charge Jamie filed with the EEOC. I was in charge of the company investigation and talked to Hamilton, Chuck Singleton, and several employees who worked with Jamie. Exhibit 6 is a copy of the report we did on the investigation.

Yes, Hamilton was investigated once before for a complaint about inappropriate behavior toward female employees. Exhibit 7 is a copy of the report we did on that investigation, in which we found no evidence to support the employee's complaint, and so we filed the matter as "unsubstantiated." We did, however, also include a requirement that Hamilton enroll in an outside vendor's training program called "Sexual Harassment/Hostile Work Environment Claims—How to Recognize and How to Avoid." Hamilton's file shows that he successfully completed that course in April YR-2.

During my tenure as human resources director, several probationary employees were not hired as full-time employees after completing the probationary period. Jamie is the only one who was fired before the sixty-day period ended.

I certify that the above is a true and accurate transcript of the deposition of Michelle Johnson taken this 18th day of August, YR-1.

Michele Johnson

DJ Sullivan

D.J. Sullivan
Certified Court Reporter

DEPOSITION OF JANET LONG

My name is Janet Long, and I have worked for Pinnacle Packaging Products since August 2003. John Hamilton is the warehouse manager, and Chuck Singleton is the foreman for two packaging lines. I have worked for Singleton since I was hired, and he always has treated me fairly.

In May YR-2, Jamie Taylor was hired to work on my packaging line. All new employees are assigned to an experienced worker for training during the first week. Jamie was assigned to me for training. Jamie is not a strong woman and had problems lifting some heavy packages. However, she learned the job quickly and tried hard to do the job and keep the line moving. Sometimes Singleton would stop and help Jamie for a few minutes. I never heard Singleton criticize Jamie during the first week, and I told Singleton that Jamie could work without my help the next week.

Some of the employees were planning on going out for drinks that Friday to celebrate Singleton's birthday. I have two children at home and did not stop for a drink. To my knowledge, the party was uneventful because I did not hear any stories on Monday.

Jamie was working on her own after the first week. At times, you can see what other employees are doing. Jamie appeared to be working hard, but a new employee usually cannot keep up with a more experienced employee. Jamie still had some problems with heavier boxes, but that also improves over time.

We are entitled to two, fifteen-minute breaks during the day and thirty minutes for lunch. Employees are expected to use the bathroom on a break, but we can leave the line if things slow down to go to the bathroom or to get a drink of water. We do not have to punch a time clock for any breaks.

It is not unusual for employees to stretch a break by a few minutes. Singleton will make a comment if the breaks are abused. Jamie is very friendly and talked to anyone who was in the area. She frequently took more than fifteen minutes for a break, but it seldom was more than twenty minutes.

John Hamilton walks through the warehouse several times a day. It seemed as though Jamie and Hamilton always had something to say to each other. They never talked long, but Hamilton talked to Jamie more than the rest of us.

Jamie complained to me about Singleton many times before she was fired. Jamie felt like he always watched her and picked on her for any little thing. Jamie was not the best employee, but she was trying hard and getting better. Jamie never said anything to me about Hamilton asking her out or bothering her.

Jamie was verbally reprimanded by Singleton for her appearance three different times. I cannot remember the exact dates. The first time was a hot day in the warehouse, and Jamie had rolled up her sleeves and tied a knot at the bottom of her T-shirt. Jamie was showing a lot of skin and drawing the attention of the guys on the line. Jerry Black was working next to Jamie, and he was making some comments. I could not hear what Singleton said, but Jamie untied the knot and rolled down her sleeves.

The second incident occurred about one week later. Jamie came to work wearing a T-shirt that said "If you can read this, you're staring." Black made a comment about being a slow reader, and I told him he was illiterate and not a slow reader. Hamilton walked past and saw Jamie's T-shirt. I could not hear the comments, but Hamilton, Black, and Jamie were laughing. Things seemed to have settled down when Singleton came around. I could tell that he was not pleased with Jamie. After her next break, Jamie was wearing the T-shirt inside out.

The third incident occurred on another hot day in the warehouse. Jamie must have held her head under a faucet because her hair and T-shirt were wet when she returned from lunch. Once again, Black had some comments, and I told him he needed to be hosed down. Singleton showed up a few minutes later. I could not hear what he said, but I could tell by his facial expressions that he was not pleased.

I know that Singleton gave Jamie several write-ups and that she went to Hamilton's office to talk to him and sign the paper. Jamie was upset when she came back to the line, but we never talked about what was said. It seemed like nothing serious happened in Hamilton's office because Jamie and Hamilton continued to exchange greetings and talk when he walked past the line.

I was surprised when I learned that Jamie was fired. Other probationary employees have had problems, and all of them were allowed to complete the sixty-day period.

I certify that the above is a true and accurate transcript of the deposition of Janet Long taken this 18th day of August, YR-1.

Janet Long

D.J. Sullivan

D.J. Sullivan
Certified Court Reporter

EXHIBITS

Exhibit 1

DISCIPLINARY ACTION

Date: _5/25/YR-2_____

Employee: Jamie Taylor_____

Evaluation: Employee is working slowly and not meeting quotas_____

_____Employee is spending too much time away from work station_____

_____

_____

_C Singleton_____   _John Hamilton_____
Foreman   Manager

Employee Comments:_____

_____

_____

_Jamie Taylor_____
Employee

Exhibit 2

DISCIPLINARY ACTION

Date: 6/4/YR-2

Employee: Jamie Taylor

Evaluation: Employee was 10 minutes late today

Employee has dressed inappropriately on 2 different dates

Employee is slow worker

C Singleton
Foreman

John Hamilton
Manager

Employee Comments: _____

Jamie Taylor
Employee

Exhibit 3

DISCIPLINARY ACTION

Date: 6/19/YR-2

Employee: Jamie Taylor

Evaluation: Employee was 20 minutes late today

  Not meeting quotas

  Employee is spending too much time away from work station

_____   _____
              Foreman   Manager

Employee Comments: _____

_____

_____

_____
              Employee

Exhibit 4

STATE OF NITA

DARROW CIRCUIT COURT

IN RE: THE MARRIAGE OF	:	
NANCY HAMILTON and	:	CAUSE NO. YR-2 CIVIL 812
	:	
	:	
JOHN HAMILTON	:	
Defendant	:	

TEMPORARY RESTRAINING ORDER

This matter has come before the court on the Petition for Restraining Order filed by Nancy Hamilton on March 3, YR-2. The court has reviewed the affidavit supporting the Petition and now GRANTS the relief requested.

IT IS NOW ORDERED that John Hamilton vacate the premises known as 1624 Oak Street, Nita City, and remain away from that residence until further order of court.

IT IS FURTHER ORDERED that John Hamilton refrain from contacting Nancy Hamilton in any fashion until further order of court.

IT IS FURTHER ORDERED that John Hamilton not enter the Nita City Food Mart, the place of employment of Nancy Hamilton, until further order of court.

IT IS FURTHER ORDERED that John Hamilton not follow, stalk, or in any manner threaten or harass Nancy Hamilton until further order of court.

ENTERED this 3rd day of March, YR-2

_____
Judge, Darrow County Circuit Court

Exhibit 5

Excerpt from Pinnacle Packaging Policies Manual

Pinnacle Packaging Products Prohibited Harassment Policy

Prohibited Harassment

Pinnacle Packaging Products is committed to providing a work environment free of harassment. Pinnacle maintains a strict policy prohibiting sexual harassment and harassment because of race, color, sex, sexual orientation, gender identity or expression, religion, national origin, age, disability, or any other basis protected by applicable law. All such harassment is prohibited. Pinnacle's anti-harassment policy applies to all persons involved in the operations of the company, including applicants, and prohibits harassment by any employee of Pinnacle Packaging Products, including managers and coworkers.

Sexual Harassment Defined

Federal law defines sexual harassment as unwanted sexual advances, requests for sexual favors, or visual, verbal, or physical conduct of a sexual nature when:

- submission to such conduct is made a term or condition of employment; or

- submission to or rejection of such conduct is used as a basis for employment decisions affecting the individual; or

- such conduct has the purpose or effect of unreasonably interfering with an employee's work performance or creating an intimidating, hostile, or offensive working environment.

State and local law definitions of sexual harassment include various forms of offensive behavior. The following is a partial list:

- Unwanted sexual advances.

- Offering employment benefits in exchange for sexual favors.

- Making or threatening reprisals after a negative response to sexual advances.

- Visual conduct: leering, making sexual gestures, displaying of sexually suggestive objects or pictures, cartoons, or posters.

- Verbal conduct: making or using derogatory comments, epithets, slurs, sexually explicit jokes, comments about an employee's body or dress.

☐ Verbal sexual advances or propositions.

☐ Verbal abuse of a sexual nature, graphic verbal commentary about an individual's body, sexually degrading words to describe an individual, suggestive or obscene letters, notes, or invitations.

☐ Physical conduct: touching, assault, impeding, or blocking movements.

☐ Retaliation for making harassment reports or threatening to report harassment.

Pinnacle's policy also protects employees from harassment by vendors or clients. If harassment occurs on the job by someone not employed by the Company, the procedures in this policy should be followed as if the harasser were an employee of the Company.

It is unlawful for males to sexually harass females or other males, and for females to sexually harass males or other females.

Other Types of Harassment

Prohibited harassment on the basis of race, color, sex, sexual orientation, gender identity or expression, religion, national origin, age, disability, or any other basis protected by applicable law, includes behavior similar to sexual harassment such as:

☐ Verbal conduct such as threats, epithets, derogatory comments, or slurs;

☐ Visual conduct such as derogatory posters, photography, cartoons, drawings, or gestures;

☐ Physical conduct such as assault, unwanted touching, or blocking normal movement;

☐ Retaliation for making harassment reports or threatening to report harassment.

Pinnacle's Complaint Procedure

Pinnacle's reporting procedure provides for a prompt, thorough, and objective investigation of any claim of harassment or discrimination. If the Company determines that prohibited activity has occurred, it will take appropriate remedial action. The discipline will be commensurate with the severity of the offense. Appropriate action will also be taken to deter any future prohibited activity. All reported incidents of harassment or discrimination will be investigated. Designated representatives of the Company will promptly undertake an effective, thorough, and objective investigation of the allegations. When the investigation is completed, a determination regarding the allegations will be made and communicated to the person who filed the report as soon as practical.

An individual subjected to what he or she believes is sexual, racial, or other improper harassment should immediately tell the harasser to stop the unwanted behavior and/or immediately report that behavior, preferably in writing, to the human resources director. If any further incident(s) of harassment occur, the incident(s) must be immediately reported.

If an employee becomes aware of harassing conduct engaged in or directed toward a Pinnacle Packaging Products employee, the employee should immediately report that information, preferably in writing, to the human resources director.

Pinnacle strictly prohibits retaliation against any person by another employee or by the Company for using this complaint procedure, reporting harassment, or for filing, testifying, assisting, or participating in any manner in any investigation, proceeding, or hearing conducted by a governmental enforcement agency. Prohibited retaliation includes, but is not limited to, termination, demotion, suspension, failure to hire or consider for hire, failure to give equal consideration in making employment decisions, failure to make employment recommendations impartially, adversely affecting working conditions, or otherwise denying any employment benefit.

Any person who is found to have engaged in unlawful harassment is subject to disciplinary action up to and including discharge from employment. A person who engages in harassment may be held personally liable for monetary damages.

Pinnacle does not consider conduct in violation of this policy to be within the course and scope of employment or the direct consequence of the discharge of one's duties. Accordingly, to the extent permitted by law, the Company reserves the right not to provide a defense or pay damages assessed against an employee for conduct in violation of this policy.

Exhibit 6

MEMO TO: File

FROM: Michelle Johnson

RE: Complaint of Sexual Harassment by Jamie Taylor

DATE: August 6, YR-2

Former employee Jamie Taylor (terminated June 22, YR-2) filed a complaint with the EEOC alleging that employee John Hamilton, her supervisor in the packing room, had sexually harassed her and that her termination was in retribution for her refusal to accede to his demands for dating, sex, or both.

I investigated this matter by collecting information from:

John Hamilton—warehouse manager

Chuck Singleton—warehouse foreman

Lisa Roberts—co-worker of Taylor's on packing line

Jerry Black—co-worker of Taylor's on packing line

Hamilton denied that he had ever harassed Taylor or asked her out on a date, except as a joke and during some good-natured banter.

Singleton corroborated Hamilton's recollection in that he (Singleton) had never observed any inappropriate behavior or touching by Hamilton towards Taylor. Singleton says that if anything it was the reverse: Taylor seemed to be flirting with Hamilton and trying to get him interested.

Lisa Roberts declined to discuss the matter. She said that she was too good a friend of Taylor's and did not want to get either Taylor or Hamilton in trouble—"let sleeping dogs lies" were her words.

Jerry Black said that in his opinion the kind of flirting that always went on in the packing room was what everyone was used to, and Hamilton's participation in it seemed to him to be just a question of "the boss trying to fit in"—nothing more. He also said that he thought there was something odd about Taylor being fired so early in her employment here, because to his view she did not perform any worse than others in tardiness, length of breaks, inappropriate comments, or dress, etc.

Given Black's comment, I re-interviewed Hamilton and Singleton on the reasons for their decision to terminate Taylor, and they were adamant and convincing in their position that she was terminated for repeated tardiness and other incidents for which she had received disciplinary write-ups.

Conclusion: Taylor's complaints are unfounded and unsubstantiated. File closed.

Exhibit 7

MEMO TO: File

FROM: Michelle Johnson

RE: Complaint of Sexual Harassment by Lisa Roberts

DATE: February 27, YR-2

Current employee Roberts has filed an oral complaint with this office alleging that her supervisor, John Hamilton, told her that she could get a promotion if she "played ball with him," which she alleges constituted a sexual overture. She further alleges that when he said this to her, during a work-progress review session with him in his office, he put his hand on her knee and rubbed it. She further alleges that this incident followed other times when she claims Hamilton flirted with her when passing her station on the packing line—but she gave no specifics in my interview with her, nor did she add any detail beyond the behavior she initially complained about.

I have interviewed Hamilton about this. He says that Roberts misunderstood him. He did tell her that she would be eligible for a promotion if she, in his words, "tried hard to learn the ropes of mid-level management" from him and Chuck Singleton (her immediate supervisor). As to inappropriate touching, Hamilton said that while he was talking with Roberts during the review session, he tripped over a leg of his office table and fell towards her, and in steadying himself he may have accidentally touched her leg or knee.

Conclusion: I find Hamilton's recollection to be more credible than Roberts's. Accordingly, the complaint is ruled unfounded. As a precaution against future incidents, Hamilton will be required to attend a sensitivity training session.

Exhibit 8

Equal Employment Opportunity Commission

Person Filing Charge	Jamie Taylor
This Person	☒ Claims to be aggrieved
	☐ Is filing on behalf of another

Pinnacle Packaging Products Inc.
1 Industrial Way
Nita City, Nita

Date of Alleged Violation	5/15/YR-2
Place of Alleged Violation	Nita City, Nita
Charge Number	YR-2-03782

Notice of Charge of Discrimination

(See EEOC "Rules and Regulations" before completing this Form)

You are hereby notified that a charge of employment discrimination has been filed against your organization under:

☒ Title VII of the Civil Rights Act of 1964

☐ The Age Discrimination in Employment Act of 1967

☐ The Americans with Disabilities Act

☐ The Equal Pay Act (28 U.S.C., Sect. 204(d) *Investigation will be conducted concurrently with our investigation of this charge.*

The boxes checked below apply to your organization:

☐ No action is required on your part at this time.

☒ Please submit by **8/17/YR-2** a statement of your position with respect to the allegation(s) contained in this charge, with copies of any supporting documentation. This material will be made a part of the file and will be considered at the time that we investigate this charge. Your prompt response to this request will make it easier to conduct and conclude our investigation of this charge.

☐ Please respond fully by ____ to the attached request for information which pertains to the allegations contained in this charge. Such information will be made a part of the file and will be considered by the Commission during the course of its investigation of the charge.

For further inquiry on this matter, please use the charge number shown above. Your position statement, your response to your request for information, or any inquiry you may have should be directed to:

Terry Mattoon
Commission Representative
555-4444
Telephone Number

☐ Enclosure

Basis of Discrimination	☐ Race	☐ Color	☒ Sex	☐ Religion	☐ Nat. Origin	☐ Age	☐ Disability	☐ Retaliation	☐ Other

Circumstances of Alleged Violation	Claimant claims she was sexually harassed and propositioned by her supervisor, John Hamilton, and that her termination was in retaliation for her refusal of his sexual advances.

Date	7/17/YR-2	Name/Title of Authorized EEOC Official	Terry Mattoon	Signature	*Terry Mattoon*

Exhibit 9

Pinnacle Packaging Products, Inc.

One Industrial Way

Nita City, Nita 99991

August 11, YR-2

Ms. Terry Mattoon

Equal Employment Opportunity Commission

22 Constitution Plaza

Nita City, Nita

Dear Ms. Mattoon:

I am writing on behalf of Pinnacle Packaging Products Inc., in response to your correspondence of July 17, YR-2, in which you provided to us a Notice of Charge of Discrimination by Ms. Jamie Taylor.

Pinnacle Packaging categorically denies that Ms. Taylor was sexually harassed by any employee of Pinnacle, or that her termination was in retaliation for any action by Ms. Taylor, as she claims. Ms. Taylor was terminated via proper procedures under Pinnacle's hiring and employment policies; the termination was made during her initial probationary period, during which she (a) showed herself unsuited to the position for which she was hired, and (b) acted in disregard of Pinnacle's work rules and regulations, despite fair and repeated warnings.

If you have any further questions concerning this unfounded allegation, please feel free to contact me.

Sincerely,

Michele Jennson

Exhibit 10

Equal Employment Opportunity Commission
Notice of Right to Sue
(Issued on request)

To:	Ms. Jamie Taylor 1234 Main Street Nita City, Nita	From:	Equal Employment Opportunity Commission 22 Constitution Plaza Nita City, Nita

☐ On behalf of a person aggrieved whose identity is confidential (29 C.F.R. 1601.7(a))

Charge Number	YR-2-03782	EEOC Representative	Terry Mattoon	Telephone Number	555-4444

(See additional information attached to this form)

TO THE PERSON AGGRIEVED: This is your NOTICE OF RIGHT TO SUE. It is issued at your request. If you intend to use the respondent(s) named in your charge, YOU MUST DO SO WITHIN NINETY (90) DAYS OF YOUR RECEIPT OF THIS NOTICE: OTHERWISE YOUR RIGHT TO SUE IS LOST.

☒ More than 180 days have expired since the filing of this charge

☐ Less than 180 days have expired since the filing of this charge, but I have determined that the Commission will be unable to complete the process with 180 days from the filing of the charge.

☒ With the issuance of this NOTICE OF RIGHT TO SUE, the Commission is terminating its process with respect to this charge.

☐ It has been determined that the Commission will continue to investigate your charge.

☐ ADEA: While Title VII and the ADA require EEOC to issue this Notice of Right to Sue before you can bring a lawsuit you may sue under the Age Discrimination in Employment ct (ADEA) any time 60 days after your charge was filed until 90 days after you received notice that EEOC has completed action on your charge.

 ☐ Because EEOC is closing your case, your lawsuit under the ADEA must be brought within 90 days of your receipt of this notice. Otherwise, your right to sue is lost.

 ☐ EEOC is continuing its investigation. You will be notified when we have completed action and, if your notice will include notice of right to sue under the ADEA.

☐ EPA: While Title VII and the ADA require EEOC to issue this Notice of Right to Sue before you can bring a lawsuit you already have the right to sue under the Equal Pay Act (EPA) (You are not required to complain to any enforcement agency before bringing an EPA suit in court). EPA suits must be brought within 2 years (3 years for willful violations) of the alleged EPA underpayment.

I certify that this notice was mailed on the date set out below.

On behalf of the Commission

1/19/YR-1	Terry Mattoon
Date mailed	

Enclosures:
    Information Sheet
    Copy of Charge

CC: Respondents

Exhibit 11

Diagram of Pinnacle Warehouse

Legend: 1 = Taylor's initially assigned station   2 = station to which Taylor was moved on May 18, YR-2   Packing Lines =

Diagram of Pinnacle packing room

Preliminary Jury Instructions

Duty of Jurors

You have been selected as jurors and have taken an oath to well and truly try this case.

During the trial, there will be times when you will be allowed to separate, such as recesses and lunch periods. When you are outside the courtroom, you must not talk about this case among yourselves or with anyone else.

During the trial, do not talk to any of the parties, their lawyers, or any of the witnesses. If anyone makes any attempt to talk to you concerning this case, you should report the fact to the court immediately.

You should keep an open mind. You should not form or express an opinion or reach any conclusion in this case until you have heard all of the evidence, the arguments of counsel, and the final instructions as to the law.

Issues for Trial

The plaintiff, Jamie Taylor, was hired by the defendant, Pinnacle Packaging Products, as a probationary employee for a sixty-day period. The plaintiff was fired before the end of the probationary period. The plaintiff contends that she was fired because she refused to date the warehouse manager, John Hamilton, who made the ultimate decision to terminate her employment.

The defendant denies that Hamilton made advances toward the plaintiff and contends that the plaintiff was fired for her poor job performance. The defendant also contends that it has a company policy prohibiting sexual harassment in any form and that the plaintiff failed to follow the company policy and report any harassment.

Preponderance of the Evidence

When I say that a party has the burden to prove an issue by a preponderance of the evidence, I mean by the greater weight of the evidence. A greater number of witnesses testifying to a fact on one side, or a greater quantity of evidence introduced on one side, is not necessarily of the greater weight. The evidence given upon any fact that convinces you oat strongly of its truthfulness is of the greater weight.

Credibility of Witnesses

You are the sole judges of the credibility of "believability" of each witness and the weight to be given to his testimony. In weighing the testimony of a witness, you should consider his relationship to the plaintiff or to the defendant; his interest, if any, in the outcome of the case; his manner of testifying; his opportunity to observe or acquire knowledge concerning the facts about which he testified; his candor, fairness, and intelligence; and the extent to which he had been supported or contradicted by other credible evidence. You may, in short, accept or reject the testimony of any witness in whole or in part.

Concluding Instruction

After I complete these preliminary instructions, the plaintiff and the defendant will have the opportunity to address you in an opening statement. Following the opening statements, first the plaintiff will present evidence and then the defendant will present evidence. After all the evidence has been presented, the parties again will have the opportunity to address you with their final arguments. At the conclusion of this case, I will give you the final instructions to guide your deliberations and assist you in reaching your verdict.

Final Jury Instructions

Burden of Proof

When I say a particular party must prove something by "a preponderance of the evidence," or when I use the expression "if you find," or "if you decide," this is what I mean: When you have considered all the evidence in the case, you must be persuaded that it is more probably true than not true.

Cautionary Instruction on Reasonableness of Defendant's Action

In deciding the plaintiff's claim, you should not concern yourself with whether the defendant's actions were wise, reasonable, or fair. Rather, your concern is only whether the plaintiff has proved that the defendant was terminated her because of sex.

Title VII

The plaintiff claims that she was discharged because she failed to submit to the sexual advances of her supervisor, John Hamilton. To succeed on this claim, the plaintiff must prove the following elements by a preponderance of the evidence:

1. She is a member of a protected class, a female;

2. Her job performance met the defendant's legitimate expectations;

3. She suffered an adverse employment action, a discharge; and

4. Another similarly situated individual who was not in the protected class was treated more favorably.

If you find that the plaintiff has proved each of these items by a preponderance of the evidence, then you must find for the plaintiff. However, if the plaintiff has not met her burden of proof, then you must find for the defendant.

If you find that the plaintiff's discharge was motivated by both (1) her refusal to accept sexual advances from a management employee of the defendant and (2) the plaintiff's poor job performance, then the plaintiff is entitled to prevail on her claim unless the defendant proves by a preponderance of the evidence that it would have discharged the plaintiff regardless of whether the alleged improper sexual advances did or did not occur.

Affirmative Defense

The employer has an affirmative defense to a Title VII claim if it had a policy against any form of sexual harassment and/or discrimination. That policy must be made known to the employees and must include a procedure for filing any complaints of discrimination.

If you find that the defendant had a policy against any form of sexual harassment and/or discrimination and that the plaintiff unreasonably failed to follow the company procedures, then your verdict should be for the defendant.

The defendant has the burden of proof on its affirmative defense.

Damages: General

If you find that the plaintiff has proved her claim against the defendant, then you must determine what amount of damages, if any, the plaintiff is entitled to recover. The plaintiff must prove her damages by a preponderance of the evidence.

If you find that the plaintiff has failed to prove any of her claims, then you will not consider the question of damages.

Compensatory Damages

You may award compensatory damages only for injuries that the plaintiff has proved by a preponderance of the evidence were caused by the defendant's wrongful conduct.

Your award must be based on evidence and not speculation or guesswork. This does not mean, however, that compensatory damages are restricted to the actual loss of money; they include both the physical and mental aspects of injury, even if they are not easy to measure.

In calculating damages, you should not consider the issue of lost wages and benefits. The court will calculate and determine any damages for past or future lost wages and benefits. You should consider the following for compensatory damages, and no others:

The mental and emotional pain and suffering that the plaintiff has experienced. No evidence of the dollar value of mental and emotional pain and suffering has been or needs to be introduced. There is no exact standard for setting the damages to be awarded on account of pain and suffering. You are to determine an amount that will fairly compensate the plaintiff for the injury she has sustained.

Proximate Cause

Proximate cause is that cause that produces the injury complained of and without which the injury would not have occurred.

Deliberations

When you retire to deliberate, select one of your number as the foreperson. After you have reached unanimous agreement on your verdict, the foreperson must date and sign the verdict form.

VERDICT FORMS

UNITED STATES DISTRICT COURT

NORTHERN DISTRICT OF NITA

DARROW DIVISION

Jamie TAYLOR,   :
Plaintiff   :
v.   :   CAUSE NO. YR-1 cv 321
                                        :
PINNACLE PACKAGING PRODUCTS   :
INC.,   :
Defendant

VERDICT FORM

WE, THE JURY, find in favor of the Plaintiff, Jamie Taylor, and against the Defendant, Pinnacle Packaging Products Inc., and assess damages in the amount of:

Dollars ($_____).

_____

Foreperson

_____

Date

UNITED STATES DISTRICT COURT
NORTHERN DISTRICT OF NITA
DARROW DIVISION

Jamie TAYLOR,	:	
Plaintiff	:	
v.	:	CAUSE NO. YR-1 cv 321
	:	
PINNACLE PACKAGING PRODUCTS	:	
INC.,	:	
Defendant		

VERDICT FORM

WE, THE JURY, find in favor of the Defendant, Pinnacle Packaging Products Inc., and against the Plaintiff, Jamie Taylor.

_____

Foreperson

_____

Date